Astronomy Now!™

A Look at
MARS

Mary R. Dunn

PowerKiDS
press
New York

W9-CFB-704

Dedicated to my son, Sean

Published in 2008 by The Rosen Publishing Group, Inc.
29 East 21st Street, New York, NY 10010

Copyright © 2008 by The Rosen Publishing Group, Inc.

All rights reserved. No part of this book may be reproduced in any form without permission in writing from the publisher, except by a reviewer.

First Edition

Editor: Amelie von Zumbusch
Book Design: Greg Tucker
Photo Researcher: Nicole Pristash

Photo Credits: Cover, pp. 5 (main), 13, 21 (main) by Photodisc; p. 5 (inset) © MPI/Getty; p. 7 (main) Shutterstock.com; p. 7 (inset) Digital Vision; p. 9 (main) © NASA/JPL/University of Arizona; p. 9 (inset) © NASA/JPL-Caltech/Cornell; pp. 11, 13 (top), 15, 17 (main) © Getty Images; p. 12 (left) © NASA/Steve Lee University of Colorado/Jim Bell Cornell University; p. 12 (right) © NASA/ESA/The Hubble Heritage Team (STSci/AURA)/J. Bell (Cornell University)/M. Wolff (Space Science Institute); p. 13 (bottom) NASA Headquarters-Great Images of NASA (NASA-HQ-GRIN); p. 15 (inset) © NASA/JPL/ASU; p. 17 (inset) © NASA/JPL-Caltech/Cornell/U.S. Geological Survey; p. 19 © ESA/DLR/FU Berlin (G. Neukum); p. 21 Courtesy NASA/JPL-Caltech.

Library of Congress Cataloging-in-Publication Data

Dunn, Mary R.
  A look at Mars / Mary R. Dunn. — 1st ed.
      p. cm. — (Astronomy now)
  Includes bibliographical references and index.
  ISBN-13: 978-1-4042-3828-2 (library binding)
  ISBN-10: 1-4042-3828-X (libray binding)
  1. Mars (Planet)—Juvenile literature. I. Title.
  QB641.D86 2008
  523.43—dc22

                                        2007005255

Manufactured in the United States of America

Contents

The Red Planet

The planet Mars has always held much mystery. For example, people have long wondered about the planet's color. Even from Earth, Mars looks red. It is often called the red planet. **Scientists** now know that iron oxide, or rust, in its soil makes Mars red. However, long ago, Mars's red color made people think of blood and war. Therefore, they named the planet for Mars, the Roman god of war.

Over the years, people have wondered if anybody lives on Mars. Many people have written stories about Martians, or people from Mars, who want to take over Earth.

People once thought the deep lines that you can see on Mars were waterways that were dug by Martians. *Inset:* You can see the rusty color of Mars's soil in this close-up picture.

Mars's Place in Our Solar System

Mars is the fourth planet from the Sun in our **solar system**. It is the last of the solar system's four terrestrial, or Earth-like, planets. The terrestrial planets are fairly small and rocky. The planets that lie past Mars are large and made mostly of gas.

Mars travels around the Sun in an almost circular orbit, or path. It takes Mars 687 days, or one Martian year, to travel around the Sun in its orbit. Earth's year is 365 days. That means a Martian year is almost twice as long as a year on Earth.

Three other terrestrial planets, Mercury, Venus, and Earth, lie between Mars and the Sun. *Inset:* Mars, seen here, is the last of the terrestrial planets.

7

Mars's Land and Atmosphere

Mars has two parts, the southern **hemisphere** and the northern hemisphere. The southern hemisphere has high landforms. It is old and rocky. The northern hemisphere has lower landforms. It has fewer craters, or large bowl-shaped holes that form when big rocks crash into a planet. This makes scientists think the northern hemisphere formed later than the southern hemisphere.

Mars's **atmosphere** is not good for living things. The air on Mars is filled with carbon dioxide, a gas that is unsafe for people and animals to breathe. Mars is also very cold. It is generally about -81° F (-63° C) there.

Victoria Crater lies near Mars's equator, the line that breaks up its two hemispheres. *Inset:* Cape St. Mary, seen here, is part of the rim of Victoria Crater.

Volcanoes

Mars has several very high mountains. Some of these mountains form a place called the Tharsis Ridge. The Tharsis Ridge is about 17 miles (27 km) high. A **volcano** called Olympus Mons lies near the Tharsis Ridge. It is the largest volcano in the whole solar system. Olympus Mons is about 341 miles (549 km) wide and 14 miles (22.5 km) high. Olympus Mons is an **extinct** volcano.

Near Olympus Mons is a big cliff. Some scientists believe that, long ago, Mars had an ocean that wore away the rock and formed the cliff.

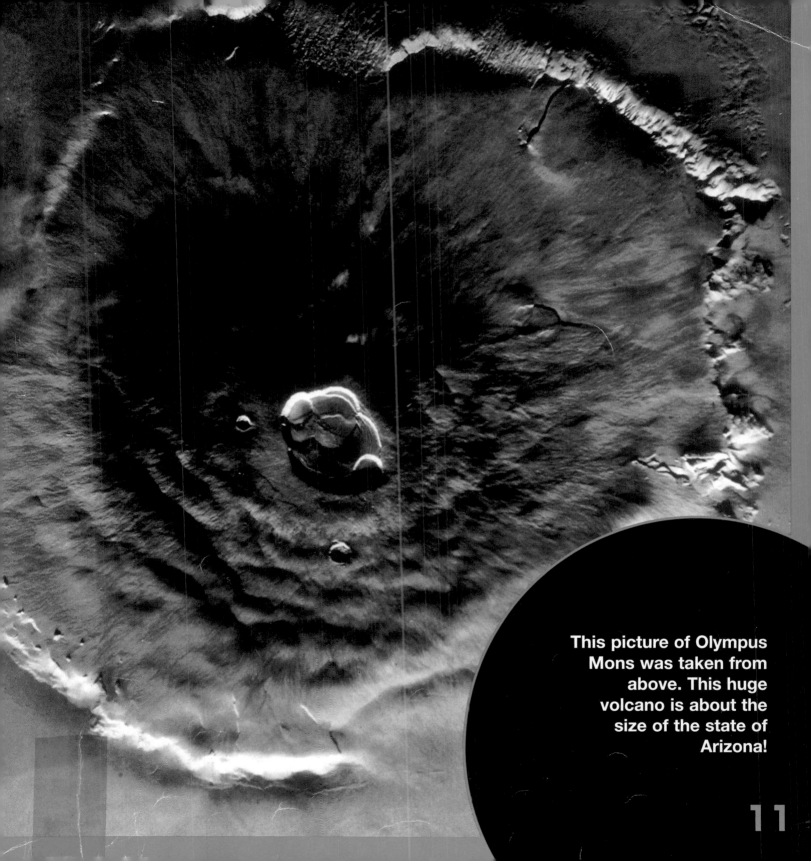

This picture of Olympus Mons was taken from above. This huge volcano is about the size of the state of Arizona!

Cool Facts

Polar Ice Caps

Mars has ice caps, or huge sheets of ice, at its poles. These ice caps get smaller in summer but grow again in winter.

Mars has dust storms. The spacecraft *Mariner 9* had to wait one month for a dust storm to stop to get a clear view of Mars.

Dust Storm

Scientists have found some dark sand dunes on Mars that are the shape of candy kisses.

Mars's moons, Phobos and Deimos, are named for two of the sons of Ares, the Greek god of war.

A Mars Timeline

2004 – The rovers *Spirit* and *Opportunity* land on Mars to study the planet.

1975 – Scientists send off the spacecraft *Viking 1* and *Viking 2*. The spacecraft land on the planet, take pictures, and study Mars.

1971 – The spacecraft *Mariner 9* begins orbiting Mars and taking pictures of the planet.

1877 – Scientist Asaph Hall discovers Mars's moons, Deimos and Phobos.

Fun Figures

A person who weighs 50 pounds (23 kg) on Earth would weigh about 19 pounds (9 kg) on Mars.

One day on Mars is 24 hours and 37 minutes long.

At the closest point in its orbit, Mars is still 128 million miles (206 million km) from the Sun.

Canyons and Dunes

Along with volcanoes, Mars has giant **canyons**. The largest canyon, Valles Marineris, is about 1,864 miles (3,000 km) long and 372 miles (600 km) wide. It is much bigger than Earth's Grand Canyon. Some scientists think floods of water formed Valles Marineris. Others believe the **crust** of Mars broke and formed the canyon. They think Mars's crust broke because the planet cooled after it formed.

Mariner 9, a spacecraft that orbited Mars, found a field of sand dunes. Sand dunes are hills of sand that were piled up by the wind. The sand dunes on Mars are much like Earth's sand dunes.

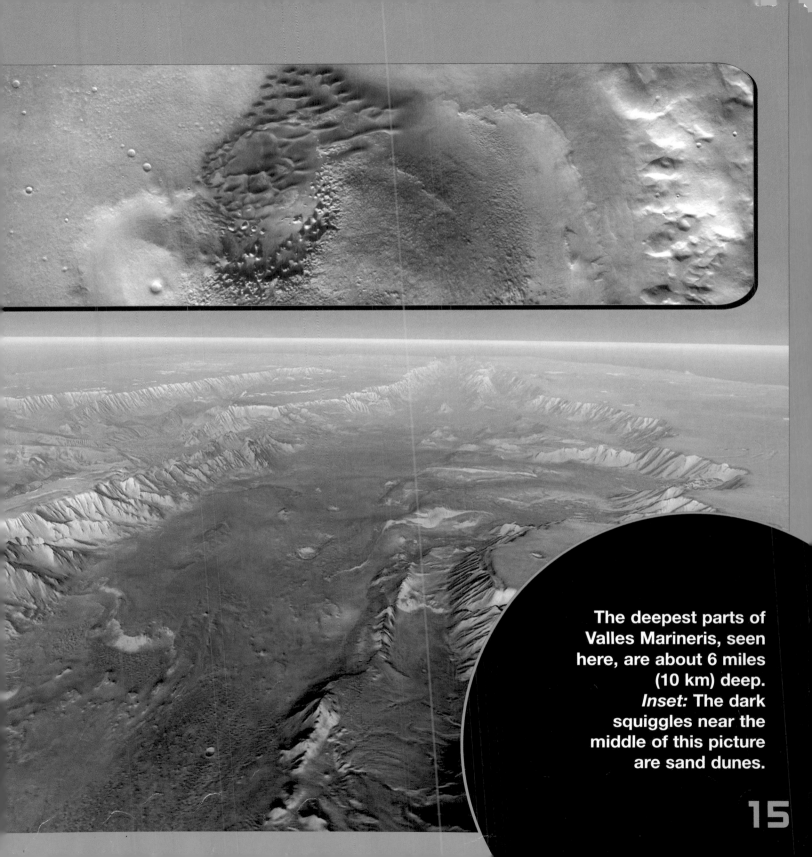

The deepest parts of Valles Marineris, seen here, are about 6 miles (10 km) deep. *Inset:* The dark squiggles near the middle of this picture are sand dunes.

Water on Mars

Scientists have long looked for running water on Mars. In 2004, **rovers** landed on Mars. One rover found rocks that had **minerals** found only in water. The rover also took pictures of small rocks that scientists think could have been formed only by water coming out of the ground. Scientists named some of the stones after kinds of ice cream, like Mudpie and Cookies and Cream.

In 2006, scientists studied pictures of Mars that a spacecraft took in 1999, 2001, and 2005. The 2005 pictures showed new trails of matter that were almost certainly left by moving water. This means Mars sometimes has running water!

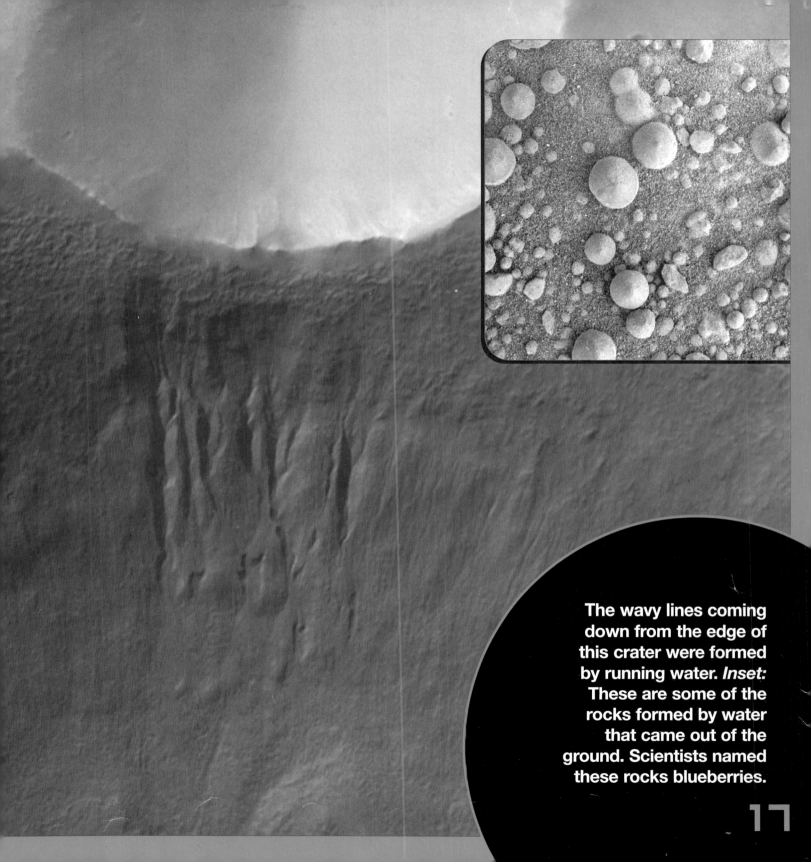

The wavy lines coming down from the edge of this crater were formed by running water. *Inset:* These are some of the rocks formed by water that came out of the ground. Scientists named these rocks blueberries.

Phobos

Mars has two moons. Some scientists think the moons are pieces of rock that were left over after Mars formed. Other scientists think the moons were objects that Mars drew into its orbit.

One of Mars's moons is called Phobos. It is covered with craters like those on Earth's Moon. It takes Phobos 7 hours and 39 minutes to orbit Mars. Phobos gets pulled about 6 feet (2 m) closer to Mars every 100 years. Millions of years from now, Phobos may get too close to Mars. If that happens, Phobos could be ripped apart or crash into the planet.

Phobos has many craters. Phobos's biggest crater is called Stickney. Stickney is on the left side of Phobos in this picture.

Deimos

Mars's other moon is called Deimos. Deimos travels more slowly in its orbit than Phobos. It takes Deimos 30 hours, or one and a quarter Martian days, to orbit Mars.

Deimos looks smooth and black and is only about half the size of Phobos. Scientists think Deimos may be made of rock and ice. Like Phobos and Earth's Moon, Deimos has craters. Its biggest crater is 1.4 miles (2.3 km) across. Deimos looks like it has fewer craters than Phobos does. This is because many of Deimos's craters are filled with dust called regolith.

This drawing shows Mars being orbited by its two moons. Phobos is on the inside and Deimos is on the outside. *Inset:* Deimos, seen here, orbits Mars at about 1 mile per second (1.6 km/s).

Scouting Trips to Mars

Scientists are planning scouting trips to Mars. They want to know if there was ever life there. If Mars once had living things, scientists want to know what made life on the planet die out.

Scientists plan to send a spacecraft called *Phoenix* to Mars. *Phoenix* will dig into the icy parts of the planet to find out about the history of water on Mars. After that, NASA hopes to set up a lab rover on Mars. The lab rover will test the planet for the best places for spacecraft landings. Someday people might at last visit the mysterious red planet!

Glossary

atmosphere (AT-muh-sfeer) The gases around an object in space.

canyons (KAN-yunz) Deep, narrow valleys.

crust (KRUST) The outside of a planet.

extinct (ek-STINKT) No longer shooting up melted rock.

hemisphere (HEH-muh-sfeer) Half of a round object.

minerals (MIN-rulz) Natural things that are not animals, plants, or other living things.

rovers (ROH-vurz) Small moving objects used to travel around planets and moons in space.

scientists (SY-un-tists) People who study the world.

solar system (SOH-ler SIS-tem) A group of planets that circles a star.

volcano (vol-KAY-noh) An opening in a planet that sometimes shoots up hot, melted rock called lava.

Index

Web Sites

Due to the changing nature of Internet links, PowerKids Press has developed an online list of Web sites related to the subject of this book. This site is updated regularly. Please use this link to access the list: www.powerkidslinks.com/astro/mars/